Instructor's Manual for

COMMUNICATING EFFECTIVELY IN ENGLISH:

ORAL COMMUNICATION FOR NON-NATIVE SPEAKERS

SECOND EDITION

Patricia A. Porter
San Francisco State University

Margaret Grant
San Francisco State University

 HEINLE
CENGAGE Learning™

Australia • Brazil • Japan • Korea • Mexico • Singapore • Spain • United Kingdom • United States

HEINLE
CENGAGE Learning

ISBN-13: 978-0-534-17269-5
ISBN-10: 0-534-17269-5

Heinle
20 Channel Center Street
Boston, MA 02210
USA

Cengage Learning is a leading provider of customized learning solutions with office locations around the globe, including Singapore, the United Kingdom, Australia, Mexico, Brazil, and Japan. Locate your local office at **www.cengage.com/global**

Cengage Learning products are represented in Canada by Nelson Education, Ltd.

Visit Heinle online at **elt.heinle.com**

Visit our corporate website at **www.cengage.com**

Printed in the United States of America
8 9 10 11 12   17 16 15 14 13

CONTENTS

INTRODUCTION: GENERAL SUGGESTIONS

We suggest you begin your course planning by reading the Preface of the textbook, which will give you a general idea of the major assignments and goals as well as information on the content of the text proper and the appendix. Teachers who have used the first edition will find that the Preface describes major changes that have been made in the second edition. We would like to stress again the importance of an experiential approach to learning and of classroom activities which promote learner involvement and interaction. This will mean assigning the text and most activities as homework and then using class time to review important concepts and to complete the activities which involve speaking and listening.

A new feature of the second edition is the <u>For Discussion</u> section. In some cases (e.g., p. 20), these questions review content presented in the section immediately preceding them. You can thus use the questions as a way of covering the material: students can read the section as homework and then go over the discussion questions in class. In other cases (e.g., p. 6), the questions ask about personal experiences and have no "right" answers. In this case, you will need to review the material in addition to covering the questions in some way.

Whichever type of questions they are, we can offer these suggestions:

1. You'll get better discussions if the students "prepare" for them as homework. This could mean either making notes in preparation to discuss the questions or actually writing out complete answers.

2. You'll get more active participation and more oral practice by all the students if you review the questions in small groups. One way is to divide the class up in groups and have each group be responsible for <u>one</u> question. Give the groups five minutes or so to discuss and prepare their answers and choose reporters. Then the reporters can present the answers to the class, standing up and facing all the class. (This improves audibility and intelligibility and gives additional practice in public speaking.)

    Another possibility is to put the class in groups and have each group do <u>all</u> the questions. A disadvantage to this approach is that you will have to allow more time for the group work. Also, in most cases it is repetitious for all the groups to report on all the questions. We suggest you assign each group one question to report on even though they will have discussed them all. Students can provide additional or conflicting ideas after the assigned group reports. (For more information on group work procedures, see the section on Group Work in this introductory part of the manual.)

3. You can cover the questions in a traditional teacher-fronted discussion with no prior group work. You may have to do this for some sets of questions if time is short, but keep in mind that the group work provides the students with additional opportunities for oral practice.

COURSE PLANNING

We have used the book to cover a semester-length course, for which it provides ample material. Whatever the length of your course, you will obviously choose to emphasize some areas more than others according to what you individually believe to be important. However, for those of you who might like some guidance in this regard, we provide a possible schedule at the end of this introductory section.

ORAL PRESENTATIONS

Coping with Student Anxiety

Although some students feel comfortable speaking in front of a group, most of your students will experience anxiety to one degree or another while in front of the class. For this reason, we have designed the speaking assignments to progress from the least threatening format (a brief presentation as a team) to the most complex (an individual persuasive presentation). In addition, we have provided activities that allow students to get to know each other and that allow them to practice and prepare for each main speaking activity. We believe that the better the students know each other and the more they can prepare for the activity, the more confident they will be.

By discussing communication anxiety in Unit 1, students will learn that others share their nervousness and that public speaking fears are normal. You can help to decrease students' feelings of stress in a number of ways. You should establish a classroom environment in which students are mutually supportive and helpful. One way you can do this is by encouraging students to know each other's names and learn personal information about each other. Also you can have students work together in small groups or pairs as frequently as possible.

2

Another way you can decrease students' anxiety is by giving them as many opportunities as possible for oral participation in the class. In this way they will get used to hearing themselves speak and further increase their confidence to express an idea in English. The activities in this book and the suggestions in this manual will help you to maximize these speaking opportunities.

Your evaluation and any peer evaluation of a student's speaking effort should encourage the student by giving positive reinforcement for good features of his or her performance. Students shouldn't be made to feel overly judged and criticized by you or their classmates. (See the section on Evaluation.)

It is our experience that the majority of students are nervous at the beginning of the course, but that this nervousness subsides as students gain confidence and experience in their speaking skills. You will, however, occasionally encounter some students who experience so much anxiety about speaking that they are unable to perform some of the activities. In such cases, you should encourage such students to complete as many of the activities as possible. Later, you can try to increase the students' confidence by giving them the less threatening activities to do, such as reading aloud from the book.

Managing Your Class for Oral Presentations

Preparing for Presentations. We strongly feel that preparing for and giving a presentation should be a learning experience, not a test; we therefore encourage much advance preparation before the actual presentation. For example, even though the text contains information and activities to help students understand what appropriate and effective topics might be, we find that students still have trouble choosing and developing topics. If you decide that you want to take an active role, at least initially, in students' topic selection, we suggest that you require students to get approval of their topics before preparing a speech. In this way, you will be able to eliminate any inappropriate topics or multiple speeches on the same topic. Before getting your approval, students can bring in several possible topics and discuss them in small groups, getting feedback from their classmates.

Regarding topic development, we suggest you require students to turn in an outline of the speech (at least the main points) several days before giving the speech. As with topic selection, students can meet in small groups or with partners to get help in developing their topics before handing in their outlines. Finally, students should be

3

encouraged to practice their speeches before giving them. If class time permits, have them give their presentations in small groups before giving them to the whole class. They could also practice with you or a partner outside of class.

Scheduling Presentations. Experience has shown us that six to eight students will be able to give a presentation in one 50-minute class hour, depending on how much time between speeches is allowed for questions and/or feedback. For the group presentations in Unit 4, you may be able to schedule two or three presentations in a 50-minute class. To determine speaking order, you can simply pass around a sheet and let students sign up in the slots you have scheduled. To make the order more random, you or the students can draw numbers out of a hat for their speaking order. Students often have suggestions for other ways to decide who speaks when: ask for their preference.

If you plan to have conferences with students to view their videotaped presentations, we suggest first signing the students up for conferences, then scheduling the presentations in the exact order of the conferences. This will avoid the difficulty of hunting on the tape for the appropriate speech during the conferences.

Evaluating Presentations. Before the presentations are given, you should decide on and explain the procedures you want students to follow in evaluating each other. We suggest you begin by going over the relevant evaluation form in the unit to be sure they understand the criteria. Then explain whatever system you have devised for evaluation. You can have each student evaluated by one classmate or by several. For a three-day series of presentations you might consider having each student evaluate another on the two days when he or she isn't speaking. If you allow students freedom to evaluate whomever they wish, it may turn out that certain speakers will receive many peer evaluations and other speakers will not be evaluated. You may also wish to have immediate oral feedback on speeches. (See the section on Evaluation.)

Managing Time. Managing time during oral presentations will be one of your greatest challenges. Be sure to announce the length of the speech ahead of time. Many students will have a tendency to run over time, so it will be up to you to control this. We suggest you have a system, such as holding up a card when 30 seconds remain, and then be ruthless about cutting them off when their time is up. (Let them conclude in a sentence or two.) If you do this during the first speaking assignment, they will appreciate the importance of planning their time carefully for all assignments. Note that if you allow every speech to run over even a minute, then you have added another half a class period to your presentation time. Finally, if you are allowing time after each presentation for questions and answers or for evaluation, be sure to let the class know how much time will be allotted for this activity and stick to this limit as well.

Audiotaping and Videotaping. You may find it helpful to audiotape the oral presentations. This allows you to review each presentation for more careful analysis of content. The tape can also be the basis of conference work with you or a tutor on the student's pronunciation, grammar, or organization. Students easily get accustomed to the tape recorder and don't seem to find it threatening.

Videotaping, while more threatening, is correspondingly more valuable to students for feedback. We suggest that videotaping begin later in the semester after students have had some experience with speaking in front of the class. We generally begin videotaping with Unit 3. You may wish to make videotaping voluntary, though generally we have found that all the students want to be taped. If time allows, you can do immediate playback in the class with commentary from other students, the speaker, and you, or you can do later playback in private conferences with students, or you can do a combination of both.

On Missed Presentations. Occasionally a student who is scheduled to speak on a particular day will be absent. At the beginning of the semester you need to announce a policy regarding such absences. Your policy may vary with the activity. For example, if a student misses a formal presentation, you may allow that student to make up the activity at a later date with or without penalty. However, if the activity is a group presentation, it is difficult if not impossible for the student to make up the work and your policy may be that the student will not receive credit.

EVALUATION

Peer Evaluation

Peer Evaluation provides students with an excellent opportunity to develop their analytical skills; therefore, evaluation activities occur in every unit. You can reproduce the evaluation forms at the end of this manual for the students and you to use. We suggest that after students evaluate each other, you collect the forms for review before giving them to the speakers. If the evaluation is in some way inaccurate, let both the evaluator and the speaker know this. You may also want to have students give immediate oral feedback to speakers after the first two presentations, asking that favorable comments precede any criticism. For the most part, students respond positively to this procedure. We have found that such written and oral feedback helps students become aware of their strengths and, at the same time, identifies areas in which they need to improve.

Teacher Evaluation

We suggest evaluating and giving feedback on all student presentations during the course, but you may wish not to grade all the presentations (for example, the reports in Units 1 and 2). As far as grading is concerned, we suggest weighing oral presentations more heavily than reports and activities. For group presentations, you can assign a grade to each group member, as well as an individual grade to each of the speakers.

For the oral presentations, we suggest weighing the grade more heavily as the course progresses. In the final presentation, students should be able to show that they have learned from the course as a whole; that is, the topic should be appropriate, the content interesting and well-organized, the argument convincing, and the delivery improved.

Midterm Conferences

We recommend a brief midterm conference (5-10 minutes) with each student as an opportunity for the student to let you know how he or she thinks things are going and as a chance for you to provide feedback. It is also a good chance for the students to use the skills they learned in Unit 2 regarding conferences. You should try to have the student do most of the speaking at the conference. You can tell students to come to the conference with note cards or an outline to help them remember the points they wish to make on these topics:

1. How they feel about their progress in the class in all areas: doing group work, giving presentations, learning course content, doing evaluations, making reports.

2. Their goals for improvement in the last half of the course: what they want to work on, how the teacher can help, how classmates can help, and how they can help themselves.

3. Any questions they have about the course.

6

GROUP WORK

Students say they like group work for three reasons: they feel freer to talk in small groups (and in fact they like being forced to talk); they find their own thinking stimulated by their classmates' ideas; and they can get to know each other better. This latter advantage is especially important for the more formal speaking assignments: they report greater confidence because of familiarity with their audience. Also many students find that their oral communication class is the only time they speak English: though they hear English in classes and in the community, they use their native language to speak with their families and friends.

Guidelines for Setting up Groups

1. Keep groups small (3 or 4 persons) to ensure maximum participation.

2. Put students of different language backgrounds together if you have a heterogeneous class. Students like to hear the ideas of classmates from other cultures and this intercultural exchange is a valuable learning opportunity.

3. Put students of different proficiency levels and degrees of talkativeness together. Students probably learn more readily from their peers than from teachers. Putting a strong student in each group will increase the chances that the goals of the group work will be met.

4. Change the groups frequently, say, at least every unit. This way students will have a chance to interact with and get to know all their classmates.

5. Avoid putting close friends together in groups. A pair of buddies tends to throw off the group dynamics.

Procedures for Group Work

1. The purpose of the group work should be absolutely clear. Define the task precisely and check to make sure it is understood. We have learned the hard way that group work is a waste of time with poorly defined tasks.

2. The group or the individual members should be "accountable" in some way; for example, they should have a problem to be resolved, a checklist to be used and handed in, an outline to be written on the chalkboard, a

summary report to be given to the class, or an individual report to be given orally or in writing. Such accountability is written into the activities in the book, for the most part.

3. Announce how much time will be allowed for the group work. Of course you may find that the task will take less or more time and can modify your time limit. Then, before the time is up, give them a warning, say five minutes or so.

4. While groups are working, you should circulate to all groups to make sure they are doing the task and to give help where needed. In most cases, it will not be appropriate for you to actually participate in the group.

5. One of the few problems with group work is that the groups will not finish at the same time. For a group which finishes early, you might suggest they review their work adding greater detail (in the case of a discussion) or that they practice their report (in the case of a report back to the class). There will always be one group that needs more time (thus the importance of the five-minute warning). What you do with these early or late finishers depends on the type of work they are doing. The important thing is that you be prepared with strategies for dealing with this situation.

6. When you have one or more members of each group reporting back to the class on their group work, we suggest you have the speaker stand up. Take advantage of this opportunity to get students on their feet; audibility and intelligibility will improve as well. Students can stand near their desks but should stand so that they are facing the entire class.

Additional suggestions regarding group work will be given within the sections on the individual units and activities.

USING THE APPENDIX

The Appendix provides information and practice activities
for several common pronunciation problems. The
pronunciation exercises are not meant to substitute for a
course in pronunciation. If you have students with
pronunciation problems which impede comprehensibility, we
suggest that these students do one of the following: enroll
in a pronunciation class, work with a tutor outside of
class, or spend some time in a language laboratory.

If you wish to cover the material as part of the classroom
instruction, we suggest you use the various sections over
the first half of the semester, rather than doing it all at
once. The students should read the material at home so that
class time can be spent on practice rather than explanation.
The first section on Speaking Clearly should take about half
a class period to present and will require you to model the
first reading selection--that is, read it aloud with
appropriate pauses and have students follow along in their
books. We have included some suggestions for working with
this material on page 19 of this manual.

We have found this pronunciation material to be useful in
tutorial sessions, with students working on particular
sections that they need. You could also assign students to
record the exercises on cassette tape in the language lab or
at home.

COURSE SYLLABUS

Cover in Class	Homework

Week 1

Introduction to course
Unit 1, Activity 1
Communication Anxiety;
   For Discussion
Review Assignment
Do Assignment Survey
Review Appendix--Rate,
   Pauses, Phrase Grouping,
   Emphasis
Review Appendix Assignment

Do Communication Anxiety
   Survey; prepare For
   Discussion
Read Assignment
Read Appendix--Rate, Pauses,
   Phrase Grouping, Emphasis
Do Appendix Assignment
Read Delivering Your Report;
   prepare For Discussion

Week 2

Review Delivering Your
   Report; For Discussion
Selected Activities 2-7
Review Preparing Your
   Report
Students present Survey
   Reports

Read Preparing Your Report
Prepare Survey Report

Unit 2, read Interview;
   prepare For Discussion
Read Communicating;
   prepare For Discussion

Week 3

Unit 2, Review Inter-
   view; For Discussion
Review Communicating;
   For Discussion
Activities 1, 2, 3A
Review Developing Inter-
   viewing Skills
Activity 4
Review Assignments and
   Preparing Questions
Partners choose topics

Read Choosing between Formal
   and Informal Language;
   prepare For Discussion
Activity 3B
Read Developing Interviewing
   Skills
Read Assignments
Prepare Questions for
   Interview
Write down person, topic,
   questions for conference

Week 4

Review guidelines for
   interview and conference
Students conduct interviews
Review Paraphrasing, Spoken
   versus Written English;
   For Discussion
Activities 5-9
Students present interview
   reports

Students have conferences
Read to the end of Unit 2
Activity 5
Prepare For Discussion
Activities 7, 8, 9
Prepare oral report of
   interview and written
   report of conference

Week 5

Students finish reports
Unit 3, Give Earthquake Speech; For Discussion
Review Analyzing Your Audience, Choosing a Topic, Narrowing Topic
Activities 1, 2
Review Main Points, Sub-points, Supporting Details, Outlining
Activities 3, 4, 5

Unit 3, Read Assignment, Analyzing Your Audience, Choosing a Topic, Narrowing Down Your Topic
Activity 1
Select 2 topics
Read Organizing the Body
Activities 3, 4
Prepare outline of body
Read Transitions
Activities 6, 7

Week 6

Review Transitions Activities 6, 7
Review Preparing Your Conclusion
Activities 8, 9
Review Preparing Your Introduction
Activities 10-15
Review Using Visual Aids
Activity 16
Review Presenting Your Speech and Listening and Evaluating

Read Preparing Your Conclusion; Activity 8
Prepare conclusion
Read Preparing Your Introduction;
Activities 11, 12
Prepare introduction
Read Using Visual Aids
Activity 16
Prepare and practice speech

Week 7

Students present speeches

Activity 17
Unit 4, Read Sample Group Discussion; prepare For Discussion
Read Assignment, Finding Your Topic, Keeping Your Discussion on Track
Activity 1

Week 8

Unit 4, Review Sample Group Discussion; For Discussion
Review Assignment
Students select topics and form groups
Review Keeping Your Discussion on Track
Activity 1

Read Exploring Your Topic
Find and mark up resource materials
Read Organizing the Main Points and Selecting Supporting Details
Activities 2, 5, 6

11

Groups meet to decide on
  resource materials
Review Working with
  Outside Sources
Review Organizing Main
  Points; Activity 3
Groups meet to decide on
  Main Points
Activity 3
Review Summaries
Activity 4

Week 9

Review the rest of
  Supporting Details
Activities 5, 6
Review Planning the
  Closing, Opening and
  Transitions
Activities 7, 8, 9
Review Preparing to
  Respond to Questions,
  Preparing Your Notes and
  Visual Aids
Activity 10
Groups meet to finalize
  and practice their
  presentations

Read Planning the Closing,
  Opening, and Transitions
Activities 7, 8, 9
Read Preparing to Respond to
  Questions, Preparing Your
  Notes and Visual Aids
Activity 10

Week 10

Groups give their
  presentations

Activity 11
Unit 5, Read Introductory
Dialog; prepare For
  Discussion
Read Solving a Problem,
  Assignment, Choosing
  Appropriate Problems
Activity 1
Select 2 or 3 problems

Week 11

Unit 5, Do Introductory
  Dialog; For Discussion
Review Solving a Problem,
  Assignment, Choosing
  Appropriate Problems
Activities 1, 2
Review Gathering
  Information; Activity 3

Read Gathering Information
Activity 3
Read Organizing the Body
Prepare note cards for
  parts 1 and 2
Activity 5A
Prepare for Activity 6
Activity 7

12

Review Organizing the Body
Activities 4-8

Write out and make copies
   of outline
Read Preparing Your
   Conclusion, Preparing
   Your Introduction
Activity 9
Prepare conclusion
Activity 11
Prepare introduction

Week 12

Review Preparing Your
   Conclusion, Preparing
   Your Introduction,
   Delivering and Evaluating
Activities 9-12
Students give speeches

Practice speech

Unit 6, Read Resource
   Article; prepare
   For Discussion

Week 13

Students finish speeches
Unit 6, Review Resource
Article; For Discussion

Activity 13 (Unit 5)
Read Speaking to Persuade
   and Expressing Opinions
Activity 2

Week 14

Review Speaking to Persuade
Activity 1
Review Expressing Opinions
Activities 2, 3
Review Gathering Resource
   Material
Review Choosing Supporting
   Evidence and Appealing to
   Your Audience; For
   Discussion
Review Outlining the Body
Activities 6-12
Review Presenting Your
   Speech, Listening and
   Evaluating

Read Gathering Resource
   Material; Activity 5
Read Choosing Supporting
   Evidence and Appealing to
   Your Audience; prepare
   For Discussion
Read Outlining the Body
Activity 6
Prepare outline
Activities 8, 9
Prepare conclusion
Activity 11
Prepare introduction
Practice speech

Week 15

Students give speeches

Activity 13

UNIT 1. UNDERSTANDING YOUR AUDIENCE AND BEING UNDERSTOOD

INTRODUCTION

As a way of beginning the course, you could present the situations and the information in the introduction and elicit from the students other examples of breakdowns in oral communication. Then, you might do some warm-up activities that focus on speaking and listening to get students acquainted with each other and with the content of the course. We recommend these three:

Activity 1.   Getting Acquainted with Your Classmates

You can give the directions orally. (Students don't need their books.) It's a good idea to have with you some thick marking pens, some 6 by 9 cards or blank 8-1/2 by 11 sheets of paper to write the topics on, and some masking tape. Students can then hold the cards up or stick them to the wall in different areas of the room.

Suggested Activity.   Learning Students' Names

The class sits in a large circle (teacher included) and the student to the left of the teacher begins by saying his/her name and one relevant piece of information. (The class can decide on this: possibly country of origin, major, or hobby.) The student to his/her left then says, "This is_____ and my name is _____and I'm from_____."
This continues around the room with each student repeating all the names of the students that have already spoken (just first names are sufficient) before introducing himself/herself. They may have to ask students to repeat their names for them. The teacher will be the last person and should then be able to name each student.

Suggested Activity.   A Lecture Previewing the Course Content

To emphasize the importance of active listening in the class and to orient students to the book, you can give a brief five-minute lecture on what the book includes and ask the students to take notes. (You can easily give this lecture spontaneously by referring to the Table of Contents, focusing on the main content and the main assignments of each unit.) After the lecture, various students can put segments of their notes on the board, or you can do a quick oral check of the main points of the lecture. For a brief follow-up discussion, you could ask these questions:
    Which unit sounds the most interesting to you? Why?
    Which unit sounds the most difficult? Why?
    Which unit sounds the easiest? Why?

HOW DO YOU FEEL ABOUT COMMUNICATING?

Students can do the Personal Report of Communication Anxiety as homework, writing their responses on a sheet of paper to be handed in. You can ask them to add up the numbers they give as responses. This will give them a total between high anxiety (possible 80 points) and no anxiety (minimum score of 16 points). Whether you have the students do the profiles anonymously is up to you: if they do include their names, you will have a chance to learn about how individuals feel, and this can be helpful to you. (For example, you won't have students with high anxiety give their presentations first.) You can collect their papers and make an anonymous class profile which averages and smooths out extremes and does not cause individual students embarrassment. (You can use this as a sample presentation. See suggestions under Listening to and Evaluating the Reports.) Another suggestion is to ask the students to retake the survey at the end of the semester. You can then hand back their original responses for comparison.

For Discussion

1. One way to begin discussion of their results on the anxiety survey is to ask for a show of hands of how many placed in the HIGH range (80 to 59 points), the MID range (58 to 36), and the LOW range (35 to 16). The class might then discuss some of the high-anxiety items chosen by a majority of the class and suggest ways to help reduce anxiety.

2. Either in groups or as a whole class, students can come up with lists of costs and benefits. You can make a handout of these and give it to them to look over before each speech (focusing especially on the benefits) and they can add to it as the course progresses. Here are some examples of things our students have come up with in addition to those in the book:

Costs	Benefits
audience laughs at you	feel more comfortable next time
say something wrong	gain confidence in presenting ideas
become nervous	convince others of your ideas
not express yourself clearly	become more organized in speaking
	freely express your ideas
mispronounce words	speak more clearly
get a stomachache	bring joy to others through speaking
audience might disagree	
forget what to say next	enjoy being the center of attention
unable to reach people	not be shy anymore

LEARNING ABOUT YOUR AUDIENCE

Read over the assignment carefully with the class. You may
be able to do step #1 during one class session. Alternately,
you might brainstorm the list at the end of one class, then
take home the list of suggestions and group them in pairs or
threes of related content and prepare a handout. At the next
class, you can ask students to find a partner and then
decide on the questions they want. (We suggest you require
students to work with students they do not know.) Or you can
simply assign the questions to pairs or threes (and you can
assign the partners or team members as well). The important
thing is that the survey questions come from the students.
However, you may have to do some judicious editing. For
example, the question "What courses are you taking this
semester?" will generate a lot of data that a pair may not
be able to report on efficiently in two minutes. One student
may suggest questions that others feel are too personal to
answer in such a survey.

Following are examples of questions that our students have
used successfully for this survey:

1. What is your country of origin?
    What is your native language? What other languages do
    you speak?

2. How long have you been in the U.S.?
    Have you had any problems with culture shock or with
    acculturation?

3. Why are you here? (Why did you leave your country?)
    Will you return to your country?

4. How do you support yourself?
    Do you work? If so, what job do you have?

5. What is your major? Is it your choice?
    What is your long-range career goal?

6. How much time do you spend on homework?
    How many units are you taking?

7. Is this your first semester here?
    What is your class level?

8. How old are you?
    Do you live with your family?
    What is your position in your family?

9. What sports do you enjoy playing?
    What sports do you enjoy watching?

10. What do you do for fun? (What are your hobbies?)
    What do you wish you had more time to do?

11. What kind of food do you like?
    Do you eat American food?

12. How do you choose friends?
    What's a good way to make friends on campus?

13. Do you like music? What kind?
    Do you play a musical instrument? If yes, which
    instrument? If no, would you like to learn one?

14. Are you a religious person?
    What is your religion? (Do you belong to a religious
    community?)

Once students have decided on their partners and their
questions for the survey, they are ready to conduct it. They
will need a list of their classmates' names for the survey,
and the most efficient procedure is for you to simply type
one up and provide each student with a copy. You can double
space the names and draw lines across the page so that the
students can actually write the information they gather on
that page.

You may want to cover the following two sections (Preparing
Your Report and Delivering Your Report) before the students
do the survey. If students have an understanding of the end
product (which they will get in "Preparing"), they may do a
better job of getting the information in the survey. Doing
the section on delivery skills and the related exercises
will help them to get to know each other and give them more
experience working together, so this may also improve their
surveying skills.

PREPARING YOUR REPORT

This section provides a brief introduction to speech
preparation skills that students will be working on
throughout the course: content and organization,
introductions, conclusions, transitions, visual aids, and
note cards. When going over the material, we suggest that
you have students stand up to read the examples. (Choose
your more articulate speakers for this task.)

Although the book gives examples of charts and graphs, you
can suggest other kinds of visual aids such as short lists,
drawings, overhead transparencies, and even pictures. (One
student brought pictures to illustrate the most popular
sports.) You may have to tell students where they can get

large paper or poster board to use for visual aids as well as remind them that color is important. You can offer to provide masking tape to put up their visual aids on the board. (For your reference, visual aids are covered in detail in Unit 3.)

To encourage students' initial use of note cards with this first presentation, you may want to require them to turn in note cards immediately after their speech. A better idea would be to check their note cards before they give the speech, though this isn't always possible. They could also have their partner check their note cards.

DELIVERING YOUR REPORT

Students generally have little difficulty understanding the features of delivery; it is developing good delivery skills that is the problem. It is to be hoped that since the course does not allow time for teaching pronunciation, students with severe pronunciation problems are also taking a pronunciation class. Students with less serious problems can be given help outside of class. Your students can also review the material included in the Appendix. You can cover the material on delivery by going over the For Discussion questions. (For suggestions on procedures, see page 1 of this manual.) Questions 2, 3, and 6 are especially good for small-group discussion and reporting to the class. When covering questions 2, 4, 5, and 7 (posture, movement, vitality, spontaneity, voice control -- rate, fluency, volume, intonation) you might get an outgoing student from the class to demonstrate the wrong things to do. (That is, have the student slouch, pace back and forth, speak softly, speak too fast, etc.)

Presenting the material on delivery is a great opportunity for those of you who enjoy being hams. You can loll around in front of the class with one hand in your pocket and the other flipping the hair off your face, punctuating whatever you say with "okay" and "you know." For this great act, we suggest you choose a topic that you yourself are familiar with so that you can concentrate on the features of delivery you want to focus on. Before you begin your talk, you might list several features on the board (e.g., posture, facial expression and gestures, volume, rate) and have students give you a rating (+ -) at the end of a short segment (a minute or two); then list other features (e.g., vitality, spontaneity, sense of humor) and talk for a minute or so more and have students rate you on those. Another possibility is to focus on the four areas of delivery they will be evaluated on in this unit: volume, rate, comprehensibility, and eye contact. Students could refer to the evaluation form on page 27 as you give your model speech.

Our colleague Vicki Lasin has successfully used the following procedure for covering the delivery features. She puts the students in groups and assigns each group a delivery feature to present to the class. They read about it for homework, then give a brief presentation in three parts: they define and explain their feature, give bad examples, and then give good examples. Each member of the group participates in the presentation.

You probably won't have time to do all the activities in this section. We would suggest that you do at least one of the note card activities (5 and 7) so that students have some practice before they give their first presentations. What some teachers do is draw upon this collection of activities throughout the course -- doing some with Unit 1 and at least one "delivery" practice with each of the other units. For example, Activity 4 is a good one to get students acquainted and to practice just talking, so it is very appropriate for Unit 1. Activity 3 (gestures) and Activity 6 (vitality) might be done later in the course if these features seem a problem for your class. Activity 2 can be done just before the presentations for Unit 1 and again before the presentations in Unit 2 if it seems to help calm nervousness.

We also suggest that you work with the first part of the Appendix, "Speaking Clearly," to introduce students to these important features of speech. You can spend about fifteen minutes in class introducing the features and doing the activities in the text, then assign each student to prepare one of the idioms in the Assignment on page 226. You should model the reading of #1, "back to the drawing board," for the class. Depending on the amount of time available for this material, several procedures are possible.

1. If you have a couple of class periods to devote to this, you might have students work on their selections at home, then meet in class in groups (all those working with #2 in one group, etc.) to compare their renditions. You can go to each group and model the reading. Then students can practice together. Finally, students can read in front of the class.

2. If you have less time yet want students to stand up and perform, you can record the selections on tape yourself, deposit your tape or tapes in your language laboratory or media center, and have students listen to and mark their selection for pauses and emphasis and then practice before performing in the class. In this way, all modeling and practice take place outside class and you use class time only to perform. Another possibility is to have only a few students actually perform in class and have the rest record their responses on tape.

3. Finally, if you have only the time needed to introduce the material in class, you might consider having the students work on their own and record their readings on audio cassettes. This will serve as an excellent diagnostic for you to see which students have more serious problems in comprehensibility and will need more help from you or an outside tutor. You can give immediate feedback on the tape. (See the suggestions on page 26 in this manual about working with audio tapes.)

Activity 2.   Relaxing to Control Nervousness

As previously suggested, you might take the students through this routine just before the presentations begin. (If presentations take two days, do it both days.) Encourage them to try the breathing routine just before they get up to speak. If this activity seems to help them, do it again before the presentations in Unit 2. Our colleague Sargham Shah recommends a "visualization" technique to combat nervousness and improve performance. She asks students to close their eyes and then she guides them step by step to visualize themselves getting up, walking to the front of the room, speaking confidently and clearly, enjoying the experience and feeling comfortable while talking, then walking back to their seats and sitting down with a sense of accomplishment. Students may be familiar with this technique as it is used by athletes, and they might enjoy trying it on themselves as "Olympic speakers."

Activity 3.   Using Gestures for Expressiveness

You'll need to prepare slips of paper or index cards, each with one adjective written on it, for this activity. If you do this activity in groups of five or six, you can use the same five or six adjectives for each group. This activity can be done as a whole class, but at the beginning of the course it may be less threatening done in groups.

Activity 4. Speaking Spontaneously and Maintaining Eye Contact

This activity may be familiar to you under the name of "fluency circles." Students sometimes have difficulty understanding that 1) the initial speakers keep speaking a second and third time and that 2) they talk about the same topic. They generally like the activity and it enables them to understand clearly that the second and third time their thoughts are more focused and they have less difficulty speaking. It also makes the point that eye contact and other non-verbal feedback from the listener are important.

Some topics you might choose from are:
my favorite place in (name of your city)   pets
an important date in my life   my best teacher
keeping physically fit   cheating
managing a time schedule   smoking
my favorite place to study/to eat   being on time
my favorite class

Activity 5. Looking Up from Your Notes

The following are possible cues for the cards, but you
should tailor the cues to fit the background of your class.
For example, if your students have all been in the U.S. for
five years or more, then the first sets of cues are not
appropriate. You can copy the cues, then tape them onto note
cards (4 by 6 or larger). We suggest using two different
colors of cards so that pairs can be formed easily. (For
example, to half the class pass out blue cards with the card
1 cues on them, and to the other half pass out orange cards
with the card 2 cues. Then tell students to pair up with
someone with a different color card.) We also suggest that
you begin by demonstrating the activity with one of the
students. For a brief follow-up discussion, you could ask
what problems students had and what strategies successful
students seemed to use.

Card 1
MUCH CULTURE SHOCK/IN U.S.?
FRIENDS/THIS SCHOOL?
PROBLEMS/LIVING SITUATION?
WHAT OPINION/LOCAL PUBLIC
   TRANSPORTATION
ENOUGH EXERCISE/RELAXATION?

Card 2
ANY MISUNDERSTANDINGS/IN US?
COUSINS, RELATIVES/THIS CITY?
PROBLEMS/SCHOOL?
PROPER FOOD/REST?

WHAT OPINION/DOWNTOWN AREA?

Activity 6. Working on Vitality

As with Activity 5, we suggest that you demonstrate this
activity with a partner. You might want to perform your
demonstration twice, once with almost no vitality and once
with good vitality.

Activity 7. Working on Volume, Rate, Posture, and Eye Contact

You may want to demonstrate the different writing sizes on
the board and also demonstrate the procedure for making up
sentences based on the words on the card. You can have
students suggest another city, food, and activity, and you
can do a second example. Your coaching here is especially
important. It's a chance for a student to get on-the-spot

21

feedback. If a student's volume, posture, and eye contact are weak, ask him or her to do it again. Ask good students to do it again to serve as a positive model.

We've suggested that for additional practice students can do the activity again with their own notes. Since you may not have time for all students to speak, you can do this practice in small groups, say four or five students. That way each can get additional practice and feedback on their use of notes, volume, rate, posture, and eye contact. Students should stand while speaking to their groups. The small-group audience could jointly agree on a rating for the speaker on the four features suggested in the activity. This should be done immediately after the one-minute talk.

Following are several other activities that work on various delivery features. You could use these in addition to or in place of those in the book. For an activity in which students practice writing on the chalkboard, see page 46 of this manual.

Suggested Activity.   Semi-impromptu Talk

In this activity, students practice fluency and delivery skills in small groups. It is similar to Activity 4, but allows for some preparation and note-card use and is done in small groups rather than one-to-one. It might be more challenging for more advanced groups. This activity would also work well in Unit 5 as a practice activity on persuasiveness. Follow-up discussions could focus on features of content and delivery that made the speech persuasive.

Each student chooses a favorite place in the geographic area to recommend to classmates. It could be a place to eat (a restaurant, coffee shop, etc.), an entertainment spot (a night club, bowling alley, etc.), an outdoor spot (a favorite place to picnic, hike, swim, exercise, etc.), or even a favorite place around school. The task is to provide information about this place and to convince classmates of the benefits of going to this favorite spot.

A suggested procedure is to begin by brainstorming with the class and listing on the board the sorts of information the talk could contain. For example: where it is, what you can do there, how you discovered it, what is so special about it, why you would encourage your classmates to go there, price of admission, open hours, etc. Perhaps work through a couple of examples (e.g., a tourist spot, a familiar restaurant) to elicit these and further ideas. Then give students about five minutes to think about their place. They jot down key words or phrases on note cards to help them remember their points.

Students work in circles of five. Each student speaks for about two minutes. Encourage them to look at the different members of the group, keeping their gaze on one individual for at least five seconds before looking at another person. At the end of the two minutes, there will be a one-minute question-answer period, in which group members will ask questions about the place.

As a follow-up, you can discuss as a class what made some talks especially interesting and communicative. Speakers can get feedback on delivery using a form similar to that in Activity 7 and should also get feedback on content (e.g., Was the information clear? Interesting? Complete?).

For additional practice, groups can reform so that each person is in a group of all new members. (The easiest way to do this is for the original group to count off one through five, then reform with all 1s together, all 2s and so on.) Repeat the exercise, with each person talking on the same topic for two minutes again. This time there will be time for only one question at the end of each talk.

For follow-up you can discuss as a class:
    Was eye contact easy to maintain? Why or why not?
    How did your talk change from the first to the second group?
    Did the questions the first group asked give you good ideas for information to include during the second talk?
    What made some talks especially interesting and communicative?

Suggested Activity.   Spontaneous Story

This chain story activity practices volume, rate, posture, eye contact and fluency. You'll need to prepare slips of paper for each student in the class, each slip containing a noun, verb, or adjective. Arrange the chairs in a circle and give each student a slip of paper. Pair each student with a partner across the circle. Partners will monitor each other's volume, posture, rate of speech and eye contact.

The teacher starts the story by giving the first sentence (e.g., "It was a stormy night in November when..."). Then each student stands up to speak in turn, continuing the story. (Students can volunteer or go clockwise around the circle.) Each person should say about three sentences and must include the word on the paper. As students are speaking, others should ask for clarification or repetition, or request that others speak more loudly or slow down.

After all the students have spoken, students meet with their partners for feedback on volume, rate, posture, and eye contact, using a simple rating sheet such as the rating sheet for Activity 7.

Suggested Activity. Simplified Charades

This activity gives students practice in getting up in front of the class without having to say a single word! The class forms two teams. Each team prepares a set of cue cards. Each card has written on it a single word: an action (crying, laughing, dancing), a thing (happiness, love, war), or a quality (sad, overjoyed). Each team should invent a system to indicate nonverbally whether the actor is acting out an action, a thing, or a quality. One by one, members of alternating teams draw a card from the other team and act out the word on the card. Their own team must guess the meaning of the word the team member is acting out. Scorekeepers keep track of the time needed to guess the correct word. The team with the lower number of minutes wins.

Suggested Activity. Miming Messages

In this activity, taken from F. Klippel's book Keep Talking, students practice eye contact and build their confidence. Each student draws a card with a message written on it (sample messages follow). Students then identify their partners (cards are numbered so that there are two of each number) and they form two lines or a large circle such that partners are across the room from each other. The first student in each pair mimes the message to his or her partner. (Half the class is miming while the other half is watching.) The observing partners write down the message as they interpret it. Then the second student in each pair mimes the message on his or her card. Finally, students sit down with their partners and compare the written messages with the original messages.

Sample messages:
I'd like to go to the movies with you. Meet me at my house
  at 7 p.m.
Can I borrow your walkman? Mine is broken.
I'm having a party on Saturday. Can you come?
Could we do our homework together tonight?

LISTENING TO AND EVALUATING THE REPORTS

As a model, you can give a two-minute presentation on some information about the class that the students are not

24

reporting on. (For example, you can collect the students' scores on the Communication Anxiety Survey and summarize that information for your presentation. If you have an assistant, one of you can present the items the class feels most nervous about and the other present the items they feel least nervous about. This way the class can see the transitions between speakers. Another possible topic is data on students' visa status, length of time in the country, majors, etc. that are not included in the students' survey questions.) You can give your presentation as either a negative model or a positive model. If you have already demonstrated poor delivery skills, then there is no need to do it again. If you do the negative model at this point, however, we suggest you re-do it as a positive one. We have found that students like the opportunity to point out features of delivery and content that are a problem.

For a negative model, make your delivery exaggeratedly bad: lean on the table, don't look at the audience, leave your notes on the table or hold them up to your face, and speak very softly. Use visual aids that are too small to see. Don't organize the information well. Students should be able to tell you what was wrong. (If not, then do it again with very good delivery and ask about the contrast.) For a positive model, be sure to use note cards and a large, attractive visual. (Students may not realize that they can use large, poster-size paper that can be taped to the chalkboard.)

These survey presentations will help you diagnose problems of the class as a whole as well as individual problems. For example, the presentations will show which students need special help with pronunciation or volume, which students are especially nervous in front of the class, and which students are strong and can perhaps help out others. We suggest that you not grade these introductions. However, you should be sure to give feedback, using the form provided at the end of the unit. We also suggest that you have one or two students evaluate each speaker, assigning who will evaluate whom. Encourage them to write down one thing they liked about the presentation and one suggestion for improvement on the form.

As the speeches are given, you may want to have thirty seconds of "reaction" from classmates and you, focusing on two strengths of the presentation (since there are two speakers) and two suggestions for improvement. Also when all the speeches are completed, you may want to discuss with the class in general terms what the main strengths and weaknesses are and some remedies for improvement.

During the speeches you may wish to have the class take brief notes; after all, the purpose of the survey is for everyone to know about their classmates as background information for their future speeches. However, here you would want to encourage the class to look at the speaker as much as possible and to go for the main points, not the details. If students are held accountable for this information (perhaps by a brief quiz after all the speeches have been given), then they may be motivated to ask for clarification during the presentations. (See Unit 2, page 42, on "Asking for repetition or clarification.") If students are to take notes, you may wish to audiotape the speeches for your information; we find it is nearly impossible to manage the class, evaluate each speaker, and retain the information all at once.

Suggested Follow-up on Class Presentations

Each of the other units after this one has a follow-up report assignment. If you wish to do such a report for this unit, here are some possible assignments. They could be written, but we would recommend that they be done orally on a cassette tape, with you giving an oral response on each tape.

Tips for students when making an oral report on tape:

Use a standard-size audio cassette.
Don't record over a music tape. Use a new tape that the teacher can also record a response on.
Before handing in the tape, rewind it to the beginning of your talk.
Prepare your report by making notes. Do not write it out first. It should be a spontaneous talk. If you don't like the way it goes the first time, simply do it again until you are happy with it.
In general, these reports should be no longer than three minutes.

1. Prepare a short report in which you summarize and discuss your results on the Personal Report of Communication Anxiety. Discuss your level of communication anxiety during your survey of your classmates and during your presentation of your survey results.

2. Prepare a short report on the oral presentations focusing on these two areas:

    A. Evaluate your own presentation. How did you feel about it -- did it go as well as you expected? Better? Worse? What did you like about it? What do you want to work on next time?

B. What did you learn about effective communication from your classmates' presentations? For example, what did some speakers do that you would like to try yourself to improve your speaking? Did you learn about anything to avoid?

(Note: If you assign this topic, it is a good idea to have students hand in with the report the evaluation forms they received from their classmates and you.)

UNIT 2.   GETTING INFORMATION: INTERVIEWS AND CONFERENCES

SAMPLE INTERVIEW

The interview can be introduced in different ways. You can ask two students to perform the interview ahead of time and either audiotape or videotape them and then play the tape to the class. It is best to have non-native speakers of English on the tape; otherwise ESL students argue that the interview goes smoothly because it is so easy for native speakers. An alternative is for the teacher to do the interview in front of the class with an assistant or a student, or to have two students practice ahead of time and do the interview for the class. Students can listen to the interview twice, the first time for the general content of the interview, and the second for the answers to the discussion questions.

<u>For Discussion</u>   (See page 1 for general suggestions on dealing with these questions.)

1.   In the assignment for this unit, students are asked to prepare one or two questions about the general background of their interview partner and then some questions about the interview topic. Following are some questions of each type from the sample interview:

Background:
A.   What is your family name?
B.   What is your home country?
C.   How long have you been in the U.S.?

Interview topic:
A.   Would you like to start telling me about your problem?
B.   How do you feel about the incident now?
C.   Do you think there's anything people can do to avoid getting caught in the type of situation you found yourself in?

2.   A.   Was it a problem finding her?
     B.   I guess she was out when you got there?
     C.   What on earth did you say?
     D.   What happened after that?
     E.   Did you hear from her after that?

3. Was it a problem finding her? The interruption was polite but probably would not have been necessary if Rita had waited a little for Anna to continue.

4. Rita shows empathy for Anna by imagining how she felt in the difficult situation with her old friend. Following are the sentences that express empathy:
    A. I can imagine how that made you feel.
    B. That was pretty blunt of her. Poor you!
    C. That was really too bad.

5. Well, thanks for the interview. You never know--learning about your experience might help some of our classmates.

    The ending is good because Rita thanks Anna for the interview and then gives assurance that the topic of the interview could be a useful one for the class to know about.

6. and 7. The answers to these questions will originate from the students.

An additional question you might ask could be "What would be some good topics to be interviewed about?"

COMMUNICATING

As homework, students can read the material on "Being an Active Speaker/Active Listener" and prepare the "For Discussion" questions. You may review the material in class by going over the "For Discussion" questions, as well as by asking specific questions such as:

What should students in the U.S. do if they don't understand what the teacher is saying?

Why is it important to be a good listener?

What are some poor listening habits?

What can you do to help yourself listen actively?

Activity 1. Listening and Retelling a Story

Here is a brief story you can use. We suggest you change any parts of it that would not be relevant to your students.

Alice is now a student at (name of your school). When she was still in high school, she decided that some day she would become a doctor. So she chose biology as her major. One semester the biology classes were very full, so she took a business class so that she would have enough units. Surprisingly, she found it very interesting. Now she isn't sure if she should continue to plan a career in medicine or change over to the business field.

Activity 2. Listening and Taking Notes

Following is a short speech that could be used for this activity. It would be a good idea to put the speech on note cards, so that the students see the instructor follow the procedures recommended to them.

Every day you listen to other people speak--family members and friends, co-workers and bosses, classmates and instructors, people on the radio and TV, as well as other people you may happen to come across. Sometimes, for one reason or another, you don't listen to these people too carefully. But I would like to make the point that most of the time you can benefit by paying close attention.

First of all, sometimes certain information is necessary to you, and you can end up in trouble if you don't listen. Suppose one of your parents or your roommate reminds you to take your key since he or she plans to be out when you come home. You are used to that person being home and don't pay attention when the advice is given. Later you find yourself locked out for several hours, a trouble you could have saved yourself if you had simply paid attention. Or, your instructor may announce a quiz for the next week, but you are talking to your neighbor at that time. The result is that you don't study and end up getting a D on the quiz.

Secondly, you can learn something new that interests you or that is useful to you. You may want to attend a concert but have decided not to go because you think it will cost too much. You learn from the radio that a certain organization has some reasonably priced tickets for sale and are able to get one. Another situation could take place on the tennis court. A partner may give you a tip to help you improve your serve, and, as a result of making the suggested change, your game becomes a lot better.

Thirdly, you may learn something about others that enables you to help them and thus also improves the quality of your relationship. You might hear a classmate or a co-worker telling someone where he or she lives. You realize that the person lives very close to you and you mention it to the person. Later you become good friends as you alternate driving each other to work or school. Or, you might hear a classmate tell the teacher that her eyesight is getting worse and that she can't see the board too well. You might be able to help this classmate by letting her look at your notes and thus feel good about what you are doing.

In conclusion, I've tried to show you three ways in which you can benefit by playing close attention when people are speaking. You can save yourself some trouble, you can learn something useful, and you can be helpful to others who need some assistance. I'm sure now that you realize the benefits, you will all do your best to become active listeners.

Choosing between Formal and Informal Language

You may review this material as you cover the "For Discussion" questions or, in addition, you might ask the following questions:

What are some occasions when formal language is used in the U.S.?

What are some occasions when informal language is used in the U.S.?

What should you do if you are not sure about the appropriate language level for the situation you are in?

Activity 3. Reporting on Informal Expressions

A. A few additional expressions you might include in your list are:

Informal	Formal
split	leave
bomb	fail
crash a party	join in without being invited
You bet	Of course
I'll buy that	I'll accept that
He's a hell of a guy	He's an admirable person

31

Developing Interviewing Skills

Students will have the opportunity to prepare open-ended and closed questions when they get ready to conduct their interviews, but at this point you could ask them to suggest additional questions to those in the text in order to make sure they understand the concept. As homework, students should also be encouraged to learn the expressions presented for ways to get additional information, ask for repetition and clarification, and restate and interrupt. Go over the brief dialogs (pages 41-43) in class, with students taking the two parts or with you taking one of the parts.

Activity 4. Practicing Interactive Listening

This activity requires groups of three. Should the number of students not be divisible by three, the instructor or an assistant might join in to make up the number. If there is one extra student, the extra student can forego being a speaker and alternate the roles of listener and observer with two of the other students in a four-person group. Some possible topics are:

> Your weekend plans
> A course you like
> Your best vacation
> Your favorite place to study

Assignment: Interviewing a Classmate and Reporting on Your Interview

You may wish to review the topics that students choose to be interviewed about by having them write them out and hand them in, or you may circulate around the room as students are deciding on their topics and ask them about their topics. Those students you don't get to or who haven't decided when you talk to them can be asked to inform you of their topic before they leave. You should warn students against choosing a topic that is too large, such as comparing the lifestyle in their own country with that in the U.S. Encourage them to choose topics about which they can supply some specific details. Following are kinds of topics that students have used successfully:

> Involvement with an activity--cooking, making
> furniture, collecting stamps, operating computers,
> flying
> Involvement with a sport/martial art--ping pong,
> tennis, soccer, karate

>
> Involvement with a fine art--painting, playing a
>   musical instrument, singing
> A special event in their life--a camping/hiking trip
> A visit to one specific place
> A student's reasons for coming to the U.S. to study
> A student's reasons for choosing his or her major

If possible, have students interview someone from another
cultural background. Also, they should not interview the
same person they worked with in Unit 1, or someone they
already know, since it is desirable for them to get to know
as many of their classmates as possible.

After the partners decide on their topics, their next step
is to prepare questions for the interviews. To facilitate
this task, students can write some possible questions for
their particular topics on the board for critique. Before
they conduct their interviews, it would be a good idea to
review the guidelines for conducting an interview. The
interviews should take about 30 minutes; that is about 15
minutes per person.

Assignment: Consulting an Instructor or Supervisor and Reporting on Your Conference

Although the text indicates that students should have a
a conference with an instructor or supervisor, the intent
is that they should consult a person in authority to obtain
some information that is useful or necessary to them.
Before the students do the assignment, have them hand in
a paper to you on which they give the topic for their
conference, the name and position of the person they will
talk to, and the questions they plan to ask. This will
enable you to make sure that their topics and questions
are appropriate. The information that students are
requesting should benefit them and should not be about a
personal matter, such as the instructor's summer vacation.
Again students can write sample topics and questions on
the board for critique before they have to hand in this
information, and you can also review with them the
guidelines for the conference. Following are some topics
that students have chosen for their conferences:

> Instructors
> Choosing the most suitable computer
> Improving English skills
> Problems with tests and methods of studying for tests
> Improving performance in a specific class
> Class requirements
> Research projects
> Getting a tutor
> Transferring credit between majors

        Bosses
New work duties
New work policies
Health benefits
Possibilities for promotion

        Foreign Student Advisor
Laws about foreign students working

        Business Owner
Requirements for starting one's own business

        Banker
Appropriate investments

Activity 5.   Practicing Paraphrasing

Students can paraphrase the sentences for homework and
review them in class. A number of students can write their
versions on the board for discussion.

Following are some sample paraphrases.

a. Anna decided to visit a friend from Taiwan who was
    living outside New York.

b. Anna thought that it might be helpful for people to
    learn about life in the U.S. before coming to the
    country.

Spoken versus Written English

This material should be assigned as homework. It is
possible to ask some specific questions to review the
material in class, such as:

    What are some differences between listening and
    reading?

    What are some of the ways in which spoken and written
    language differ?

You may also review the material through the responses to
the discussion questions.

Preparing the Oral Report on Your Interview

When students prepare the oral reports of their interviews
(and the written reports of their conferences), you can
advise them that it may be necessary to re-order the

information they obtained. The material should be
organized in such a way that the report is smooth and clear
and, therefore, their reports will not necessarily follow
the order of their notes.

Activity 6.   Speaking from a Note Card

The instructor should prepare a note card rather than use
the one in the book for this activity in order to provide a
good model for the students.

Activity 7.   Preparing and Speaking from a Note Card

A.   Following is a possible version of Rita's second note
card:

> 2.
> Went 1st to N.Y.
> 1 sem. at City Univ.
> Friend outside N.Y.
> Decided to visit

Activity 8.   Comparing Notes and Paragraphs

1.

> 1.
> Carlos - new empl. - acc. co.
> Needs info on probat. period
> Interviews - sup. Ms. Brown

> 2. Prob. period = 6 mos.
> On probat when 1st hired
> Work evaluated
> Not permanent 'til after probat.
> Must have satis. record

```
┌─────────────────────────────────────────┐
│  3.  Evaluation                          │
│     ─────────────                        │
│  accuracy and efficiency                 │
│  How fast learn new tasks                │
│  Attitude toward  work                   │
│  Relationship w/ co-workers              │
│                                          │
└─────────────────────────────────────────┘


┌─────────────────────────────────────────┐
│  4.                                      │
│                                          │
│  Carlos' response:                       │
│    Everything evaluated                  │
│    Will do his best.                     │
│                                          │
│                                          │
└─────────────────────────────────────────┘
```

2.   Following is a possible written summary:

Carlos, a new employee in an accounting company,
recently interviewed his supervisor, Ms. Brown, about
the probationary period in his office. He learned that
the probationary period was six months and that he
would not be considered a permanent employee until
after he had completed this period with a satisfactory
work record. Ms. Brown informed him that he would be
evaluated in different ways. The company would
consider the accuracy and efficiency of his work, the
speed with which he learned new tasks, his attitude
toward his work, and his relationships with co-
workers. Carlos responded to Ms. Brown that it seemed
that everything he did would be evaluated but promised
to try his best to prove himself a good employee.

Activity 9.   Preparing a Spoken and a Written Advertisement

You can assign part 1 of this activity to be handed in on
cassette tapes and just have a few students give their
reports in class. When recording their advertisements,
students should talk from note cards rather than from a
script that is written out. They will have to bring their
note cards to class since they will not know which students
will be called on to present their advertisements.

Listening and Evaluating

For this presentation, we suggest that you give an overall grade of +, √., or -, and then a letter grade for the remaining speeches. In addition to doing your own evaluations, it is a good idea to have two students evaluate each presentation. If you wish to grade students on how they fill out evaluation forms for subsequent speeches, you may want to point out that filling out the forms for this presentation offers them a good opportunity for practice.

You may wish to assign your students a self-evaluation oral report at the end of this unit. Here is a suggestion for setting it up.

Prepare an oral report on your tape. On this tape, please talk about points A and B. You can also discuss points C and D if you wish.

A. Your oral presentation (report on an interview).
   Compare it to your first presentation. For example, what was easier? Harder? Were you more confident? Less nervous? Better prepared? What did you improve on? How do you feel about the evaluation form and suggestions?

B. Your conference with a teacher/boss/advisor.
   Tell who you talked to, where, and on what topic. Then discuss the conference -- how it went. Here are some questions to give you ideas. Were you comfortable? Did your questions get the information you wanted? Was the person you talked to friendly? Cooperative? Any problems? How could this experience help you prepare for another conference?

C. Your interview of your classmate.
   For example: Were your questions okay? Did you have trouble understanding him/her? Did the interview go well? Did you enjoy it? What did you do especially well?

D. Being interviewed by your classmate.
   For example: Did you pick a good topic? Were you comfortable? Was it easy for you to answer the questions? Did you like being interviewed?

UNIT 3.   PROVIDING INFORMATION: INSTRUCTIONS AND DEMONSTRATIONS

SAMPLE SPEECH

It would be better for students to hear the speech "Are You Prepared for an Earthquake?" presented from note cards than to read it in the text. This would be a good task for an assistant if you are fortunate enough to have one. You can use the outline given before the speech as a visual aid and refer to the various points where they are indicated in square brackets. The other suggested visual aids are a flashlight and battery-operated radio.

For Discussion (See page 1 for general suggestions on dealing with these questions.)

1. The speaker attracts the listeners' attention by asking the audience about their whereabouts on a specific date when a major earthquake occurred in San Francisco. She uses the personal pronouns "I" and "you."

2. The plan for the speech is to discuss what people should do before, during, and after an earthquake.

3. A. There are a number of things you can do before an earthquake occurs.

   B. Now that you have made all the necessary preparations, what should you do when you feel the earth starting to quake?

   C. Now that I have told you how to make preparations for an earthquake and what to do during an earthquake, I will continue with some advice about what you can do after the earth stops quaking.

4. The speaker brings in personal comments as follows:

        Great Britain, where I was raised
        the shelves crammed with books over my desk
        Our family had absolutely no idea how serious
            the San Francisco earthquake was
        My son was one of those who had this experience

5. The speaker gives a summary of the main points, refers back to the San Francisco earthquake mentioned in the introduction, makes an appeal to the audience, and uses a quotation for a strong closing.

6. The visual aids the speaker uses are an outline of the speech, a flashlight, and a battery-operated radio.

Finding a Topic and Analyzing Your Audience

Your first task after presenting the earthquake speech is to go over the requirements for the speaking assignment for this unit and make sure that students understand them. Since they have already learned something about their audience from the class survey and interview reports, they should be encouraged to choose topics that are likely to interest their classmates. Depending on the make-up of your classes, you may wish to place some restrictions on the topic choice. Students can be asked not to choose topics that might cause embarrassment, e.g. How to have safe sex, or that might promote violence, e.g. How to use a handgun. Otherwise, they should conform to the suggestions in the text for choosing and narrowing a topic so that they can provide sufficient relevant details within the time limit.

Activity 1. Deciding on Appropriate Topics

Audience: general adults
Time limit: 10 minutes
+   how to read palms
-   how to set a VCR to record a program (Each brand
        is programmed differently; the procedure is
        complicated; it's too hard to see the machine.)
-   how to play baseball (It isn't possible to explain
        all aspects of the game in ten minutes.)
-   how to use a word processor (It isn't possible to
        do this in ten minutes; it requires equipment.)
+   how to set up a personal budget

Audience: general adults
Time limit: 5 minutes
+   how to do a magic trick
-   how to play the guitar (It's impossible in 5 mins.)
+   how to floss and brush your teeth (only if you have
        training as a dental technician and have large
        models of teeth and brush)
+   how to write a short business letter
+   how to repot a plant

Activity 2. Narrowing Down Topics

You need to warn students ahead of time that they must have thought of possible topics by the date on which you plan to do this activity. Otherwise, they may say they can't think

of anything to demonstrate. To save time, students can do
the brainstorming for homework and bring it in to show you,
if you want to make sure that they did it.

We suggest that you keep students in the same groups for
all those activities that concern the preparation of the
students' individual speeches. Students are then familiar
with each other's topics and do not have to start thinking
about new topics each time they meet. The activities
involved for Unit 3 are 2, 5, 7, 9, 15; alternatively, you
can keep the same groups together for all the activities in
the unit. We have found groups of three to be the most
satisfactory and would definitely not recommend more than
four.

ORGANIZING THE BODY OF YOUR SPEECH

Although the steps for organizing the body of the speech
are given in some detail in the text, it would be a good
idea to go over the various steps in class using the
chalkboard or an overhead projector. Using the overhead
projector would have the advantage of allowing you to
prepare the transparencies ahead of time and would save the
time necessary to write the lists on the chalkboard. It
would also be possible to put the outline on a
transparency. If you want your students to follow a
different outlining system, then, of course, you will need
to provide them with a sample.

Activity 3. Choosing and Ordering Main Points

The item "Cost of flowers and foliage" is not directly
related to arranging flowers and therefore cannot serve as
a main point. The cost could be mentioned, however, in the
introduction or under the main point "Selecting flowers and
foliage." "Different types of containers" might serve as a
subpoint under "Selecting an appropriate vase"; it does
not relate to the topic in the same way as the other items.
The following seems to us the most logical organization for
the remaining items:

    I Selecting flowers and foliage
   II Selecting an appropriate vase
  III Preparing suitable support materials
   IV Arranging flowers and foliage

Activity 4. Choosing and Ordering Main Points and Subpoints

Here is one possibility for ordering the points, but as long as students present a logical order that they can defend, that order should be accepted.

 I Show responsibility toward your work
    Get work done on time
    Be conscientious about details
    Have regular attendance
    Be on time

 II Show initiative
     Be willing to spend your own time to try out new
        ideas
     Make independent suggestions
     Take a few calculated risks

 III Develop a cooperative attitude toward fellow
      employees
      Be friendly
      Accept help and suggestions gracefully
      Help others feel good about their jobs
      Don't complain about others

Activity 5. Evaluating the Body of Your Speech and Your Classmates' Speeches

Students should write their outlines for homework. However, for a variety of reasons such as wanting to change their topic, some students may come unprepared. We suggest that these students be put in a separate group to complete their outlines and that they be required to meet outside class to complete the activity.

Following are some questions you can use to review the material on transitions before doing the activities.

Why is it important to make clear transitions when giving a speech?

What are some helpful one-word or short-phrase transitions you can use when giving a demonstration or a set of instructions?

What are some other ways of making transitions?

Activity 6. Practicing Transitions

Some possible answers for part A are:

1. Once you have learned all about your camera, what
    else do you think you should know?
    Or
    And what do you also have to think about besides the
    camera and the lighting in order to take a good
    picture?

2. I have already explained to you how to control for the
    amount of light, so the next thing we have to consider
    is the di   is the direction of the light.

3. Now that you understand how to control for the lighting
    and how to compose a picture, the final step in the
    process is how to do a good job of actually shooting
    your picture.

Activity 7. Planning and Practicing Your Own Transitions

If students prepared outlines for Activity 5, there
shouldn't be any problem in having them do this exercise.
Part A and the note card preparation in Part B can be done
for homework.

PREPARING YOUR CONCLUSION

Here are some questions to ask in reviewing the conclusion
section:

   What is the main function of a conclusion?

   What does the first part of a conclusion usually
   consist of?

   What are some ways you can help the audience to
   remember what you said?

   How should your conclusion end?

Activity 8. Evaluating Conclusions

a. This conclusion could provide more information about
    the two techniques of self-defense, but otherwise is a
    good conclusion. It refers to a previously mentioned
    incident, makes an appeal to the audience, and has a
    strong ending.

b. This conclusion doesn't summarize the reasons why the auto mechanics course is valuable nor does it explain how the speaker has benefited from taking the course. It does make an appeal to the audience; however, the ending could be stronger.

c. A good conclusion. It summarizes the qualities needed to be a good tutor. Although it doesn't make a direct appeal to members of the audience to become tutors, it does point out the benefits that can come from tutoring and ends on a positive note.

d. This conclusion is not satisfactory. It doesn't summarize the process, mention the speaker's experience, or appeal to the audience except indirectly in the second sentence.

e. This conclusion could provide more information about what playing the anklung involves although it does indicate that you play the anklung by shaking it. The speaker points out that playing the anklung can provide the satisfaction that comes with producing a melody on a musical instrument. Therefore, this conclusion meets the criteria for being a good one.

Activity 9. Evaluating Your Classmates' Conclusions

The conclusions should be prepared at home for the group work in class.

PREPARING YOUR INTRODUCTION

To review this section, you may wish to ask the following questions:

What are some ways in which you can catch the listeners' interest?

What are some ways in which you can create a good rapport with your audience?

How should your introduction be organized?

If you use these questions and make lists of the responses on the board, then individual students could read (in random order) the introductions on pages 88-93. After each introduction, the class could review which techniques were used for rapport and catching interest, then review the organization.

Activity 12. Evaluating Introductions

Before assigning this activity, you might want to point out
to your students that a good introduction to a demonstration or instructional speech does not necessarily
require that the plan for the speech be given in detail.
The text uses the introduction to a speech on tutoring to
show students how to establish a plan for their speeches;
however, the introduction could still be considered a good
one if the speaker said, "I'm going to tell you about the
three requirements for being an effective tutor."

a. This introduction creates rapport by asking the
    audience a question and interacting with them at the
    beginning. It moves from the general to the specific
    by starting with skydiving, mentioning safety, and
    ending up with two ways to help ensure safety when
    skydiving. However, the topic statement is confusing
    in that it indicates what a good training program will
    do rather than what the speaker will demonstrate.

b. In this introduction, there is no attempt to create
    rapport with the audience, arouse the listeners'
    interest, or move from the general to the specific;
    however, the sentence given does lay out a plan for the
    speech.

c. This introduction needs a beginning sentence to
    introduce the topic, create rapport, and arouse the
    listeners' interest. The fourth sentence needs to be
    revised to clarify the speaker's purpose in giving the
    speech. A possibility might be, "I'm going to explain
    to you how this six-day-a-week program works; it has
    three parts--the work-off, the walk-off, and the weigh-
    off." The final sentence is not the topic of the
    speech and, therefore, should be discarded.

d. This is a good introduction. It creates rapport by
    including the audience at the beginning. It moves from
    the general to the specific by mentioning the problem
    of falling asleep at the beginning, then discussing
    some possible remedies, and ending up with two self-
    relaxation techniques.

e. Also a good introduction. The speaker begins with the
    general idea of an outdoor activity. Then he arouses
    interest in what he is going to demonstrate by his
    enthusiasm about kite-flying. He offers the audience a
    reason for making their own kites and then gives the
    plan for his speech.

Activity 13. Listening to and Evaluating Introductions

In order to provide a good role model, it is important that
you present the sample introductions as if you were giving
a speech and that you not simply read them out from the
teacher's manual. We would, therefore, suggest putting
them on note cards. You may wish to give the introductions
twice. If you don't want to repeat them, you can tape
yourself, rewind the tape, and allow the students to listen
to the introductions again. Then, you can stop after each
one to ask students to report on and discuss their
evaluations.

1. Today I'm going to talk about what you need to know
    before you take a picture. First, you should know
    about lighting.

Comment: This introduction needs improvement. It does
state the topic clearly and states the speaker's purpose.
But it doesn't lead into the body of the speech from
general to specific, it doesn't catch the listeners'
interest, and it doesn't create a good rapport with the
audience.

2. There are three things that you should know before you
    take a photograph. You should know as much as you can
    because most people take really bad pictures. My
    brother, for example, takes some of the worst pictures
    of anyone. So he should really be here today. I hope
    at least you take better pictures than he does. First,
    you should know about lighting.

Comment: This introduction needs improvement. It states
the topic, but in the first sentence, so it isn't organized
from general to specific, and it will be confusing for the
listeners. The story of the brother might catch the
listeners' interest, but it doesn't serve to illustrate
well the speaker's point. By using personal pronouns, the
introduction might create rapport with the audience.

3. How many of you have a camera? Probably all of you.
    But how many of you consider yourselves to be good
    photographers? Probably not many of you. The truth is
    that just owning a camera doesn't make you a good
    photographer. You need to know at least three things
    before you can take pictures, and I'd like to tell you
    about these three things today. First, you should know
    about lighting.

Comment: This introduction is good. It goes from general
to specific; it states the topic clearly; it gets the
listeners' interest; it tries to create a rapport with the
audience. It states the speaker's purpose.

4. It often happens that one takes photographs while vacationing, but more often than not, what one hopes to achieve is not what one actually gets. This is because most individuals are not accomplished photographers. They haven't acquainted themselves with proper photographic techniques. If individuals are aware of just a few of these points, their photographs will certainly improve. First, one should know about lighting.

Comment: This introduction needs improvement. It uses a style more appropriate to written than to spoken English (sentence length, vocabulary, use of "one" and "individuals"). It does not catch the listeners' interest well, nor does it create a rapport with the audience. The style would probably make it difficult for the listeners to understand. It does go from general to specific and it does state the topic at the end.

USING VISUAL AIDS

To review this section, you might ask students the following questions:

What are some reasons for using visual aids when giving a speech?

What are some benefits and cautions you should consider when using the following kinds of visual aids?

physical objects	posters
handouts	overhead/slide projectors
chalkboards	cassette players

You may wish to do the following activity to give students practice in using chalkboards and posters:

The instructor draws a large circle on the chalkboard and tells the students that the circle represents the country of each student in the class, no matter what shape the country really is. The task is to use the circle to show the audience what borders the country on the north, south, east, and west. The teacher should start off the activity by showing what borders the U.S. in all four directions.

Students then take turns coming to the board to tell about their own countries. Throughout their brief presentations, they should face and maintain eye contact with the audience. Any student who faces the board, turns toward it when moving from east to west or vice versa, or talks to the chalkboard for more than a word or two may be asked to repeat.

Activity 16. Choosing Appropriate Visual Aids

Following are suggestions for visual aids for the topics given in this activity:

Business letter--handout, overhead projector, chalkboard
First aid--a classmate, splints, bandages, as indicated
Greek folk dance--several classmates or the whole class
Brush your teeth--a large-scale model of the teeth, a large-scale brush, and floss

LISTENING AND EVALUATING

You may wish to have students hand in their outlines or note cards so that you can check them and possibly grade them. We normally assign a letter grade for this and subsequent speeches.

If you have a video camera available (see the section on videotaping in the introduction to this manual), you can tape these speeches and afterwards meet and view the tape with students individually to evaluate their performance. These evaluations could also serve as midterm conferences in which you discuss the students' progress thus far in the course and give suggestions on what they need to work on.

As for the previous speeches, we recommend that each student be evaluated by two classmates as well as yourself. If you videotape students, you might want to replay one of the early speeches (or better yet, a tape of an anonymous student from another class or previous semester) and review with the class how to write a helpful and appropriate evaluation. From this point on, you may also wish to grade students on how they complete the evaluation forms; they can find out their grades from the classmates who receive the forms.

Activity 17. Reporting on an Instructive or Demonstration Speech

You may want to have students turn in this report on a cassette tape. (For guidelines, see the suggestions on page 26 of this manual.) An alternative would be to have them give an evaluation of their own speech.

UNIT 4. PROVIDING INFORMATION: GROUP DISCUSSIONS AND PRESENTATIONS

SAMPLE GROUP DISCUSSION

Students can read the discussion and prepare the For Discussion questions for homework. We suggest that you ask three students to read the discussion aloud to the class.

<u>For Discussion</u>

1. In his role as moderator, Raul opens the discussion, he asks direct questions to ensure equal participation ("What about you, Najwa?"), and he manages the discussion by asking questions (as just indicated, and "Anything else, Najwa?") and by summarizing ("So, let's see what we've come up with so far..."). He appears to be doing a good job: he gives others the chance to speak and he contributes his own ideas, too, and he checks to see that his summary is accurate.

2. Yes, the participation seems more or less equal. The moderator asks questions, as indicated above, and the group members ask questions, too ("But what about you, Raul?"). The moderator talks more than the other two because it is necessary in his role of managing the discussion.

3. That they are listening to each other is seen in their response to each other's comments "You've come up with some good questions," "And, like you Kenji, I'm also interested...," "I've heard people say that, too," "What do you mean?" "I see what you mean," and "Me, too."

Assignment: Giving a Group Presentation

For this assignment we suggest groups of three or four students. If possible, it is good to get students thinking ahead about their topic selection. You can even suggest to them at the beginning of the semester that they look over the topics on pages 111 and 112 and be thinking about current issues that interest them. For example, what articles in newspapers and magazines capture their attention? What interesting topics come up in their other classes? If you follow the procedures suggested in the section on Finding a Topic, you should be able to get the groups established with topics they are interested in and that the whole class is interested in.

KEEPING YOUR DISCUSSION ON TRACK

One way to approach this section is simply to elicit what the class knows about group discussion and list the principles on the board. Another way is to assign the section and Activity 1 for homework and then review the material in class by going over the questions in the activity.

Activity 1. Reviewing Some Points about Small-Group Discussions

1. Some possible points students might make about whole-class discussions are: Students may be required to raise their hands before speaking; not everyone can participate; it is often difficult for the participants to hear other speakers; there is always a leader of the discussion who often writes salient points on the board and controls who gets to speak; participants may be reluctant to share personal information with a large group, etc.

2. All the points relevant to participating fully, getting into the discussion, keeping contributions relevant and direct, showing how ideas are related, and listening actively would apply to whole-class discussions.

3. All topics are possible in small-group discussions, but those that are of a more personal nature are better in small-group discussions than in large.

4. The best number is three to five. If the group is larger than that, participation is not likely to be equal and involvement is not as good.

5. Participants should contribute to the discussion but not monopolize it.

6. Participants can ask each other questions.

7. In a small-group discussion, you can use an "opener" to get the floor. You can use simple openers such as "You know" to preface your comments, or you can use an expression such as "Could I ask" or "I'd like to comment on that."

8. The group can stay focused on the topic by preparing for the discussion and by making explicit reference to how ideas are related; when a group member begins to stray off the topic, you can ask how the point relates to the topic.

9. Showing how your point is related helps you and the other participants see how the ideas in the discussion fit together and may help you focus what you want to say. It also shows the group that you have been paying attention to and value what other members are saying. You can do this using the expressions listed under "Referring to previous ideas," "Showing agreement," and "Showing disagreement."

10. Active listeners can show the group members that they are involved by eye contact and requests for clarification, and by relating their contributions to those of others.

11 and 12. Students will have differing responses here.

13. The moderator's duties include opening the discussion, ensuring relatively equal participation, and managing the discussion, which involves summarizing from time to time and dealing with conflicts.

EXPLORING YOUR TOPIC

If your students have minimal experience working with library resources, you may wish to go over the information in Figure 4.1, pointing out the titles, the authors, the periodicals and what various abbreviations mean, such as *il*, *v*, and *p*.

ORGANIZING YOUR PRESENTATION

<u>Activity 2. Organizing Main Points for a Presentation</u>

Possible orders are:
a. number of deaths, laws, attitudes, solutions
b. childhood, work in Calcutta, winning, recent work, contributions
c. location, reasons, effects, efforts

<u>Activity 4. Summarizing Information</u>

A possible summary is as follows:

> In addition to becoming more hostile, homeless people are now reluctant to stay in shelters because of diseases there. Also, they are hesitant to accept public benefits because of the degrading way they have to wait in lines and the poor treatment they get from social workers.

Activity 5. Analyzing Supporting Details

1. <u>Examples, explanatory information</u>: If you look at this chart I've prepared,...; One reason is that...; Think of all the new jobs in the fast food industry...
   <u>Statistics</u>: 25 million in 1979 to 33 million in 1986; below the poverty level of $12,000 a year; 30 percent
   <u>Direct quotation</u>: "Experts say a growing number..."

2. ...according to Peter Jones...; Jones points out...; In Jones' own words...

3. The speaker uses a chart showing the number of poor people and how these numbers have changed over time.

4. <u>Original</u>: Experts debate the causes of homelessness, but most point to four interrelated factors....
   <u>Paraphrase</u>: There are four major causes of homelessness in America....They are:...

Activity 6. Adding Supporting Details

a. According to U.S. Social Security Administration data, as reported in the article by Jones, from 1970 to 1980, the percent rise in spending on social welfare programs was 14 percent, but from 1980 to 1985 it was only 7 percent.

b. The estimated number of homeless in 1990 was 3 million, according to Steven Manning's 1989 article in Scholastic Update.

c. According to Manning, Bush has said, and I quote, "I'd like to feel we would address homelessness with sensitivity and compassion."

d. One reason is the increasing number of homeless; the other is a change in the homeless population that has been reported by a study done at Temple University. This change is that the homeless are now younger and are members of minorities; 30 years ago they were older and white.

Activity 7. Evaluating Conclusions

a. This conclusion is effective in that it provides an adequate summary and a more or less memorable ending.

b. This conclusion offers no summary, and, while it appeals to the audience to be more sympathetic, it doesn't have a particularly memorable ending.

c. This conclusion comments effectively on what the group got out of their discussion and reading, and it has a memorable closing, but it does not summarize the main points.

Activity 8. Evaluating Introductions

a. Although this introduction is long, it grabs the listeners' attention with the description of a homeless man, it creates rapport by the numerous references to the audience ("introducing you," "you've probably," "Have you seen him?" etc.), and it makes the topic and plan clear. It is a good introduction.

b. The speaker tells who the group members are and what the topic and main points are, but fails to grab the listeners' attention or create rapport.

c. This introduction is effective: it creates rapport and interest with the poll at the beginning. It introduces the topic and plan clearly.

Activity 9. Evaluating Transitions

a. The transitions are weak. Instead of "That's it," Speaker A could say, "Now that I've told you about the four main reasons for homelessness, Nita will discuss the attitudes people have toward the homeless." Speaker B could say, "As Suzie has said, I'm going to tell you about attitudes toward the homeless."

b. The transitions are fine.

c. The transitions are weak. Speaker A could close with, "My classmate Emilios will now tell you what is causing the increase in these numbers." Speaker B could then begin with, "I'm sure you are all wondering just why these numbers are so high." The speaker could close with something like, "My classmate Kim will now tell you how people's attitudes have changed toward the ever increasing numbers of homeless people."

Activity 10. Preparing Note Cards and Visual Aids

A. Possible note cards:

---

1. 4 causes of homelessness
   (P. Jones, '89, Scholastic Update
   - poverty
   - fed. budget cuts
   - no cheap housing
   - inadequate care for
                mentally ill

---

2. First, poverty
   - more people living below
     poverty level (Jones)
   - chart: $ 12,000 = poverty
              1979 = 25 mil.
              1986 = 33 mil.

---

3. cause of ↑ poverty
         = low-paying jobs (Jones)
   Why?
   ① new jobs pay minimum
       e.g. fast food: cashiers McD.
                       cooks P.H.
   (show) 40 hrs. @ min. → below $12,000

---

4. Jones - quote
   "Experts say a growing
   number of the nation's homeless
   - maybe 30% - have jobs.
   Yet with the cost of living
   rising, these people simply
   can't make ends meet."

B. Possible visual aids: a poster with the four main
points listed; a graph like the second one accompanying
the excerpt from article 1; a poster (or the chalkboard)
showing the computation of how much someone would make
at minimum wage working 40 hours per week.

UNIT 5: PERSUADING OTHERS: SOLVING A PROBLEM

INTRODUCTORY DIALOG

The purpose of the introductory dialog is to introduce the topic of problems people encounter in daily life and the idea that there may well be solutions to these problems. The dialog also introduces the theme of conflict resolution that is used throughout the unit as the basis of a proposal speech.

For Discussion

1-4. Students' answers will vary.

5.   The techniques that Jose uses include: 1) showing support for the person with a problem ("I don't blame you," "That's a difficult situation"), 2) asking for information to clarify the problem ("Are they openly hostile?" "What did she say?"), and 3) telling her about his solution to a similar problem, indirectly suggesting a comparable remedy for her.

Assignment: Giving a Problem/Solution Speech

We have found that the most successful problem/solution speeches are those that have bearing on our students' lives. This is why we suggest thinking of a problem at school, home, work, etc. that has a realistic solution. These topics work well because the context is familar to all the students and likely to be of interest. When reading the assignment, the students may be confused regarding "counter arguments against this solution" in point 3. You can explain that this procedure is covered in the unit.

CHOOSING APPROPRIATE PROBLEMS

Regarding point 2, some teachers don't agree with our idea that the solution be one that is enforceable. We've included this requirement because it forces students to make their solutions specific and grounded in action rather than generalities.

Activity 1. Evaluating Possible Problems and Solutions

a.   If the audience includes a number of students under twenty-one, this solution is not going to be very popular. Additionally, the solution is not a very realistic one.

b.   The problem is likely to have great appeal, but both
      problem and solution should be narrowed for a 5-6
      minute speech, perhaps limited to paper or aluminum and
      glass. Also the solution is not enforceable.

c.   The problem may or may not have appeal depending on
      conditions at your school and in your city. The first
      part of the solution is not enforceable, but could be
      changed to read "Students should be required to take a
      course in self-defense." The second part of the
      solution is too vague and not enforceable.

d.   This problem may have more or less appeal depending on
      whether or not day care is a topic of interest to the
      audience. The solution would have to be stated more
      specifically (what the law is now, what changes the new
      law should include, etc.).

e.   The problem may have appeal if students attended high
      school in the U.S. The second part of the solution is
      not enforceable.

f.   The problem should be of interest if your school has a
      comparable situation. The solution is good because it
      is enforceable.

g.   The problem and solution lack general appeal; the
      solution is not enforceable.

Activities 2, 3, and 4

For Activity 2, Activity 3B, and Activity 4, it would be a
good idea to use one or two students' problems and solutions
as examples for whole-class discussion before doing the work
in small groups.

For the evaluation of students' work in progress in
Activities 2, 3, 4, 5B, 6, 8, 10, and 12, we suggest that
you set up groups that work as a team throughout the unit.
If you do this, students will be familiar with each other's
topics. Groups of three or four are a good size for this
work. Larger groups are impractical because of the amount
of time required for evaluating each group member's work.

Activity 9.   Evaluating Conclusions

a.   This conclusion makes the focus clear, motivates the
      audience by pointing out negative consequences, and
      closes with a strong statement. However, it doesn't
      indicate very clearly how the audience can request the
      change. Additionally, it deals with conflict on the

personal level only, excluding the global. Especially good: The speaker relates the content well to the audience ("all of us," "we can," etc.) and appeals to the audience's sense of economy.

b.   This conclusion starts out effectively, but gets bogged down by giving too much summary information ("we can take a course in..."). It isn't clear about what the audience is being required to do, and the quote from Maria seems a bit beside the point.

c.   This conclusion meets all the criteria. Especially good: It has a strong opening sentence, it is comprehensive in covering both personal and global conflict, it makes the benefits clear, and it has a strong closing quotation.

Activity 11.   Evaluating Introductions

a.   This introduction attracts the listeners' attention and builds rapport by involving all audience members with the dramatic statistics. It also builds credibility, but states the topic in a limited way only. It is especially good in the way it makes the audience feel the weight of the statistics.

b.   This introduction gets attention by referring to "conflict" on the board, and builds rapport with the focus on common problems; it builds credibility through the reference to the speaker's work in the counseling center and studies in psychology. The topic is clear. The introduction is especially good in the building of credibility.

c.   This introduction attracts attention with the story and builds rapport by mentioning that the experience could happen to any of us. The topic is stated clearly. The problems are that it doesn't build credibility and tells too much about the overall contents of the speech (the last four sentences). The use of the anecdote is especially good.

Activity 13.   Reporting on a Problem/Solution Speech

As with other reports, this one can also be done orally on a cassette tape. If students each evaluate two speakers they could choose the more convincing speech to write about. You might also wish to include a question asking students to react to how their own presentations went, and what they feel they need to work on for their next (and most likely final) speech.

UNIT 6. PERSUADING OTHERS: TAKING A POSITION

RESOURCE ARTICLE

This article serves as the main source of information for the sample speech in this unit which takes a position against an <u>English-only</u> amendment to the U.S. Constitution. Students should read the article and prepare the "For Discussion" questions for homework.

<u>For Discussion</u>

1. The author is strongly opposed to English-only laws.

2. A. English-only laws can abridge the rights of individuals who are not proficient in English.

   B. They perpetuate false stereotypes of immigrants and non-English speakers.

   C. Such laws are contrary to the spirit of tolerance and diversity embodied in our Constitution.

   D. Some states have laws that:
      1. restrict bilingual education
      2. prohibit multi-lingual ballots
      3. prohibit non-English government services, e.g. courtroom translation or multi-lingual emergency police lines

3. <u>Emotions</u>:

   The example of the 911 emergency dispatcher and the Salvadoran woman and her baby.

   ... the "new" Italian and Eastern European immigrants were inferior to their predecessors, less willing to learn English, and more prone to political subversion.

   The New York State Constitution was amended to disfranchise over one million Yiddish-speaking citizens.

   The California Constitution was similarly amended to disfranchise Chinese, who were seen as a threat to the "purity of the ballot box."

   ... the government sought to "Americanize" Native American Indian children by taking them from their families and forcing them to attend English-language boarding schools, where they were punished for speaking their indigenous languages.

The "sink or swim" experience of past immigrants left more of them underwater than not.

Intellect:

The history of English-only laws

The states which have English-only laws

What the various English-only laws address

Statistics showing the percentage of immigrant children performing below grade level in 1911

Statistics showing the percentage of Latinos able to speak English

Statistics about the number of immigrants on waiting lists for English classes

4. and 5. The answers to these questions will originate from the students.

Choosing a Topic and Analyzing Your Audience

First you should review the assignment, making sure that students understand what it means to take a position and support it. As regards choosing a topic, some teachers prefer that students not speak on a topic such as abortion because people already have very fixed points of view, and it is unlikely that a speaker would be able to change anyone's mind. However, other teachers feel that any topic should be permissible as long as it is presented in an acceptable and appropriate way. Obviously, you will provide the guidelines on what is appropriate for your own classes.

In order to determine their classmates' attitudes, the students can conduct a survey as indicated in Activity 1. Since each speaker's assignment is to persuade the classmates to take his or her position, you might want to make the rule that if the survey shows that a majority of the class already agrees, the speaker should change the topic and repeat the survey.

Activity 1. Doing a Survey to Determine Classmates' Attitudes

To prepare for this activity, you can have some students write their questions on the board and review whether or not they are appropriate. Students can make their own list of opinions as they talk to their classmates, or you can supply them with a list with sufficient space between the names for students to make a note of their classmates' opinions.

Activity 2. Distinguishing between Facts and Opinions

In the following list of answers F represents fact and O represents opinion: O, F, O, F, O.

Activity 3. Expressing an Opinion on Your Speech Topic

This activity provides good preparation for the speech assignment in that it gives students an opportunity to try out and evaluate the effectiveness of their arguments ahead of time. Also, the questions may give them ideas about additional information they can include to strengthen their arguments.

The text suggests that this activity be done as a whole class or in small groups. We have found that medium-sized groups of six to eight students can also work well. This size group has the advantage of providing students with a larger audience than a small group and does not take as much time as having every student speak to the whole class.

When carrying out the activity, you should ask students to set their cards aside after the five-minute preparation period and not refer to them again until it is their turn to speak. Otherwise, they will continue to work on them and not pay attention to the other speakers.

Activity 4. Organizing Reference Material

Barringer, F. (1990, February 8). Judge nullifies law mandating use of English. The New York Times National, pp. A1, B10.

Nakao, A. (1986, September 21). Battle of words heats up over "English only." San Francisco Sunday Examiner and Chronicle, pp. A1, A12.

Nichols, S. (1991). English as a symbol of American culture. English Today, 25, pp. 31-35.

Vasquez, F. (1988, February 7). The diversity of our nation
is the source of our strength. <u>Rochester Democrat and
Chronicle</u>, p. A17.

Activity 5. Evaluating Classmates' Purpose and Arguments

As we suggested in Units 3 and 5, it is a good idea for
students to remain in the same groups for the activities
that directly relate to the preparation of their individual
speeches; for this unit, these activities are 5, 7, 10, 12.

As a means of checking that the group evaluations are
working satisfactorily, you could have each group select
one of its outlines to put on the board and then go over
the group's responses to each of the questions.

For Discussion

1. Generalizations, analogies, cause-effect reasoning.
    Students may either cite the examples in the text or
    provide their own.

2. Make valid claims and support them with factual
    information and/or relevant statistics; cite authority
    figures who agree with your position.

3. Make a comparison; tell a short anecdote.

4. A speaker can provide enough background on the topic to
    inform the audience, as well as use logical reasoning
    and make appropriate appeals.

5. A speaker can do the following: bring up things that he
    or she is likely to have in common with the audience;
    appeal to values that most people share; point out how
    taking an opposing position may have undesirable results;
    show how supporting his or her position will be
    beneficial. Students may either cite the examples in
    the text or provide their own.

6. An emotional appeal aims at the audience's feelings;
    a rational appeal aims at the audience's intellect.

Activity 6. Evaluating Evidence

1. Generalization: Thousands are on waiting lists for
    English classes in New York and Los Angeles; 95% of
    first-generation Mexican-Americans are proficient in
    English, so we don't need an English-only amendment to
    the Constitution to make immigrants learn English.

Cause-effect: If English-only laws in Florida and Denver caused discrimination in the workplace, then such an amendment to the Constitution is likely to cause more widespread discrimination.

2. Showing specific knowledge of English-only laws, research in bilingual education, numbers of people on English class waiting lists, and specific cases of discrimination in states with English-only laws could all build the speaker's credibility.

3. To counter the argument that previous immigrants succeeded without bilingual education, the speaker gives examples of those who did not. She also points out that previous immigrants were preparing themselves for a different job market from the one we have today.

   To counter the argument that English-only laws promote unity and harmony, the speaker points out cases in which discrimination has already occurred and that the benefits that come from the mixing of different cultures are lost when people can no longer use their own languages in public.

   The speaker did provide convincing responses.

4. Appeal to values: Most people would agree that the opportunity to get emergency help and to get a fair trial are rights that everyone should have.

   Negative consequences: Poor and elderly immigrants would be hurt most if such an amendment to the Constitution were passed.
   Alternative approaches to problem-solving would be lost.
   Cultural traditions would diminish.

   Benefits: International affairs can be conducted more smoothly.
   International business can be carried out more easily.
   People gain a broader perspective by learning and using different languages.

5. The ideas of people being without normal social services and not getting a fair trial could be used to appeal to the audience's emotions; also people's being discriminated against at work and cultural celebrations being prohibited.

   The research on bilingual education, the statistics on immigrants who have already learned English or are on waiting lists for English classes, the arguments about international affairs and business could all appeal to the intellect.

61

Activity 8.   Practicing Transitions

Following are some possible responses:

1. What do you think might be the most harmful effect
    that an English-only amendment to the Constitution
    could have on non-native speakers of English?

2. Although English-only laws already exist that can
    deprive people of their civil rights and eliminate
    bilingual education, such laws are completely
    unnecessary.

3. Now that you have heard these arguments against
    English-only laws, let's consider the point of view of
    those who think it would be a good idea if we had a
    law than banned bilingual education.

4. In the past, a majority of jobs were blue-collar-type
    jobs which did not require a lot of skills; in
    contrast, today many of these jobs are done by
    machines, and workers need more technical skills to
    be able to get a job.

Activity 9.   Evaluating Conclusions

a. This conclusion doesn't indicate clearly that the
    speaker is concluding the speech and doesn't provide
    any summary of the main points. It does make an appeal
    to the audience and suggest a course of action, but
    does not have a strong ending.

b. This conclusion has all the characteristics of a good
    conclusion. It gives a brief summary of the most
    important points. It provides a specific action that
    audience members can take and ends with a strong
    appeal to the audience.

c. This conclusion refers to the content of the speech
    with the phrase "possible harmful effects of an English
    language amendment to the Constitution," but this
    phrase does not provide an adequate summary. The
    speaker does not propose any action, and the weak
    ending makes an ineffective appeal.

Activity 11. Evaluating Introductions

a. This introduction provides background information about the states which have English-only laws and the dates when they were passed. Being able to provide such detailed information enhances the speaker's credibility from the beginning of the speech. The specific topic and purpose of the speech are clearly stated in the last sentence of the introduction. However, this introduction makes no attempt to grab the audience's attention, nor does it establish rapport with them.

b. This introduction does attempt to build rapport by beginning with values that the audience is likely to share. However, the audience is unlikely to realize that the speaker is giving the plan for the speech in the first sentence. The speech topic and the purpose are not made clear; and this introduction makes no attempt to establish the speaker's credibility or provide any background on the topic.

c. This is a good introduction. It tells a story to enlist the audience's support. It provides background about English-only laws and makes the point that the speaker has done research in order to establish credibility. The specific topic and the purpose of the speech are clear. The plan is not given in detail but the speaker indicates that she will cover various harmful effects that an English-only amendment to the Constitution could have, thereby providing sufficient preparation for the audience.

LISTENING AND EVALUATING

Again, it would be helpful to play a videotaped earlier speech and fill out an evaluation form as a class. Students thus become aware of the specific items they need to pay attention to when evaluating classmates' speeches.

PANEL DISCUSSIONS

The kind of panel discussions we suggest also involve persuasion and, therefore, can serve as an alternative to individual persuasive speeches. Students can propose topics which can be written on the board with spaces for names of those taking a pro position on one side and a con position on the other side. We would suggest no more than three people per side, and each side should have the same number of people. Topics can be chosen from the lists in Unit 4, and the groups can use the same methods of preparation as they did in Unit 4.

You will need to review the procedures for conducting the discussions with the class and discuss the moderator's role. We suggest getting strong students to act as moderators. While the groups are preparing their presentations, you can meet with moderators, going over with them the correct pronunciation of the names of the students on the panels they will moderate, appropriate ways of presenting the topics, and the time allotments for the various parts of the discussion. Moderators should review the list of duties on page 216, as well as the suggestions for group leaders in Unit 4 on cutting off talkative group members and managing conflicts.

Unit 1   Report on Survey

Speaker _____

Evaluator _____

Topic _____

RATING SYSTEM: + = excellent
$\checkmark$ = average
− = weak

Content

_____ Introduction (or conclusion)

_____ Information

_____ Transition to/from other speaker

Delivery

_____ Volume

_____ Rate

_____ Comprehensibility

_____ Posture

_____ Eye contact

Suggestions for next presentation:

Unit 2 Report on Interview

Speaker _____

Evaluator _____

Content

_____ Introduction (background information)

_____ Focus on one main topic

Topic _____

_____ Supporting details

_____ Conclusion

Delivery

_____ Volume

_____ Rate

_____ Comprehensibility

_____ Posture

_____ Eye contact

Comments and suggestions for next presentation:

Unit 3   Instructions/Demonstration

Speaker _____

Evaluator _____

Topic _____

RATING SYSTEM: + = excellent
                √ = average
                − = weak

Content/Organization/Preparation

_____ Opening attracted listeners' attention.

_____ Topic was clearly stated in introduction.

_____ Information was easy to follow.

_____ Appropriate transitions connected the points.

_____ Speech had a suitable conclusion.

_____ Visual aids were effective.

_____ Content fit time limit.

Presentation/Delivery

_____ Eye contact

_____ Vitality

_____ Rapport with audience

VOICE CONTROL:

_____ Volume

_____ Rate

_____ Fluency

_____ Comprehensibility

Comments and suggestions for improvement:

Unit 4　Group Informative Presentation: Individual Evaluation

Speaker _____

Evaluator _____

Topic _____

RATING SYSTEM:　+ = excellent
$\checkmark$ = average
− = weak

Content/Organization/Preparation

_____ Main points were clear.

_____ Points had good supporting detail.

_____ Information was presented in the speaker's own words.

_____ Transitions from previous speaker and to next speaker were smooth.

_____ Content fit time limit.

_____ Responses to questions were clear.

Presentation/Delivery

_____ Eye contact

_____ Vitality

_____ Rapport with audience

_____ Use of note cards or outline

VOICE CONTROL:

_____ Volume

_____ Rate

_____ Fluency

_____ Comprehensibility

Comments and suggestions for improvement:

Unit 4   Group Informative Presentation: Group Evaluation

Group _____

Evaluator _____

Topic _____

RATING SYSTEM: + = excellent
√ = average
− = weak

_____ Introduction was effective.

_____ Main points were clear.

_____ Points had good supporting detail.

_____ Transitions between speakers were smooth.

_____ Conclusion was effective.

_____ Visual aids were effective.

_____ Presentation was well balanced among speakers.

_____ Presentation was interesting.

_____ Questions were answered clearly.

_____ Participation was approximately equal in the question-and-answer period.

_____ Question-and-answer period ran smoothly.

Main points of the presentation:

Comments:

Unit 5   Problem/Solution Speech

Speaker _____

Evaluator _____

RATING SYSTEM: + = excellent
$\checkmark$ = average
− = weak

Topic _____

Content/Organization/Preparation

Fill in the relevant information where spaces are provided.

_____ Introduction was appropriate.

_____ Problem was stated clearly:

_____ Problem was described adequately.

_____ Solution was stated clearly:

_____ Solution was described adequately.

_____ Arguments against the proposal were countered.

_____ Benefits of solution were clear.

_____ Speech had a suitable conclusion.

_____ Speaker answered questions well.

_____ Content fit time limit.

Presentation/Delivery

_____ Eye contact   _____ Rapport with audience

_____ Vitality   _____ Spoke convincingly

_____ Gestures   _____ Use of note cards or outline

_____ Effective use of visual aids

VOICE CONTROL:

_____ Volume

_____ Rate

_____ Fluency

_____ Comprehensibility

Overall

_____ The speech was convincing. Tell why or why not:

Other comments:

Unit 6 Persuasive Speech

Speaker _____

Evaluator _____

Topic _____

RATING SYSTEM: + = excellent

√ = average

− = weak

Content/Organization/Preparation

_____ Opening attracted listeners' attention.

_____ Background information was sufficient.

_____ Speaker's point of view was clear.

_____ Arguments were clear. List below.

1. _____

_____

2. _____

_____

3. _____

_____

_____ Evidence was convincing.

_____ Opposing arguments were countered well.

_____ Appropriate transitions were used.

_____ References to source materials were adequate.

_____ Speech had a suitable conclusion.

_____ Visual aids were effective.

_____ Content fit time limit.

Presentation/Delivery

_____ Eye contact

_____ Vitality

_____ Gestures

_____ Rapport with audience

_____ Spoke convincingly

_____ Use of note cards or outline

VOICE CONTROL:

_____ Volume

_____ Rate

_____ Fluency

_____ Comprehensibility

Comments and suggestions for improvement:

Unit 6　Panel Discussion: Individual Evaluation

Speaker _____

Evaluator _____

Topic _____

RATING SYSTEM:　+ = excellent
　　　　　　　　　√ = average
　　　　　　　　　− = weak

Content/Organization/Preparation

_____ Arguments were clear.

_____ Arguments had strong supporting evidence.

_____ Evidence was convincing.

_____ Transitions from previous speaker and to next speaker were smooth.

_____ Speaker asked relevant questions.

_____ Speaker responded to questions well.

Presentation/Delivery

_____ Eye contact

_____ Vitality

_____ Rapport with audience

_____ Spoke convincingly

_____ Use of note cards or outline

VOICE CONTROL:

_____ Volume

_____ Rate

_____ Fluency

_____ Comprehensibility

Comments and suggestions for improvement:

Group _____

Evaluator _____

Topic _____

RATING SYSTEM: + = excellent
$\sqrt{}$ = average
– = weak

_____ Introduction was effective.

_____ Arguments were clear.

_____ Arguments had strong supporting evidence.

_____ Evidence was convincing.

_____ Transitions between speakers were good.

_____ Conclusion was effective.

_____ Visual aids were effective.

_____ Presentation was well balanced among speakers.

_____ Content fit the time limit.

_____ Panel asked relevant questions.

_____ Panel responded to questions well.

_____ Participation was approximately equal in the question/answer period.

List the team's arguments:

Comments:

CPSIA information can be obtained
at www.ICGtesting.com
Printed in the USA
FFOW02n1451200913
1852FF